Wild Spirit

Anxiety Relief Patterns of Tribal Chieftains

Coloring Book For Adults

CASEY B POOLE

Wild

3... EMBRACE THE CHALLENGE!

READY YOUR COLORS AND PREPARE TO EMBARK ON AN
ARTISTIC QUEST. EACH PAGE IS A NEW ADVENTURE, A BLANK SLATE WAITING FOR YOUR
UNIQUE TOUCH. FEEL THE EXCITEMENT BUILD AS YOU CHOOSE YOUR FIRST DESIGN.

2... IGNITE YOUR IMAGINATION!

WITH EVERY HUE YOU LAY DOWN, BREATHE LIFE INTO
INTRICATE PATTERNS AND BOLD HEADDRESSES. WATCH AS YOUR STRESS FADES WITH EACH
STROKE, REPLACED BY A GROWING SENSE OF PRIDE IN YOUR CREATION.

1... UNLEASH YOUR CREATIVITY!

NOW, TAKE THE PLUNGE! LET YOUR CREATIVITY FLOW ONTO
THE PAGE. AS YOU COLOR, LET THE WORLD FADE AWAY. THIS IS YOUR TIME—CALM,
PEACEFUL, AND VIBRANT.

GO!

BEGIN YOUR JOURNEY WITH 'WILD SPIRIT: ANXIETY RELIEF
PATTERNS'

YOUR WILD SPIRIT AWAITS!

Thanks For Coloring